COMMUNICATING THE GOSPEL ACROSS CULTURES

THE AFRICAN PERSPECTIVE

REV. SAM OPPONG

Communicating The Gospel Across Cultures
by Rev. Sam Oppong

Printed in the United States of America

ISBN 9781625095466

For further information, please contact:

Rev. Sam Oppong
A. Ext. 28/21 Airport Extension
P.O. Box 1133
Sunyani, Ghana.
Tel: (Mobile) 233-208118209
Email: soppong@ymail.com

www.xulonpress.com

*To my wife, Margaret, who has supported me
throughout the ministry, and to my children, Felix,
Daniel, Priscilla, Anna, and Andrew,
for their support and prayers*

CONTENTS

INTRODUCTION

To many people, culture is associated with traditional dancing, drums, dress, music, and art. In my Ghanaian culture, when someone is referred to as "cultured," it means that he understands and has mastered his own culture and that he also knows how to communicate to others effectively and in a well-mannered way in a social context. On the other hand, when someone is referred to as "uncultured," it means he is "uncivilized."

Although the word *culture* is commonly used in our everyday language and seems to be well understood by the ordinary person, the word has been used to mean different things on different occasions. Our understanding of culture helps us to know more about ourselves and how to relate to other people. It helps us to appreciate the behavior of others, which in turn leads to the building of good relationships. If we are to reach other people and be effective communicators of the Gospel, the starting point must be our genuine desire to understand and adapt to the people's culture.

Culture has been defined as a way of life, a design for living, and the practice of traditions, to provide a few definitions. According to Dr. Louis J. Luzbetak, in his book *The Church and Cultures*, "There are no less than one hundred and sixty-four, and close to three hundred definitions of the term." He continues, "It is no easy matter. ... In fact, there seems to be as many definitions as there are anthropologists" (1970, 59). It is such a complex definition that I am going to attempt to define the term *culture* in the following chapter.

Chapter One

DEFINITION OF CULTURE

I would like to comment briefly on anthropology before moving on to the various definitions of culture. To the ordinary or average man, anthropology means the study of bones and other physical features of man. It is true that some anthropologists do such studies, but the subject is wider than that. Anthropology, as the science that provides the concepts and methods for analyzing and understanding customary ways, has been described by Dr. Louis J. Luzbetak as

> studying man as a member of a group and
> not as an individual unlike psychology and

physiology. Unlike history, biology and medi-
cine, it does not focus on my particular point
of man but takes a holistic or total viewpoint
of him, the entire man, over the entire earth
and throughout the entire history of mankind.
(1970, 23)

And anthropology has been defined by Dr. Eugene A.
Nida, in his book *Customs and Cultures*, as "the science of human culture" (1954, 25).

Generally, anthropology has been divided into two
main branches: physical and cultural. The physical
anthropologists are more interested in the physical
and biological processes of the human body in relation to cultural and historical factors; others within the
same group are more concerned about the origins and
evolution of the human body. On the other hand, cultural anthropologists study the psychological, social,
and cultural aspects of human life.

As Professor Paul G. Hiebert explains in his
book *Anthropological Insights for Missionaries*,

"Anthropology seeks to discover the interrelation-
ships between various scientific models of the human
being" (1985 23); however, for the purpose of this
book I shall limit myself to the discussion or study of
the cultural aspect of human life. Having mentioned
that, I will begin by discussing the various definitions
of culture.

Due to the complexity of humankind and human
behavior, various attempts to define culture by both
secular and Christian anthropologists have not been
easy, and the debate still continues. It is therefore no
wonder that some members of the general public have
given incorrect explanations about what culture really
means. Some explanations have been based solely on
the social, geographical and physical environment.
Some have tried to explain why others behave differently from them by using biological reasons with particular reference to their parents and where they were
born, although they may have lived and grown up in a
different environment.

We cannot deny the fact that social, geographical,

biological, and other physical factors do have an influence on our individual lives, but no factor on its own can adequately explain the phenomenon behind the human behavior of an individual or that of a community as a whole. Culture involves the whole lifestyle of the individual as a member of a community or social unit. It is the result or an outcome of the interplay of social factors.

Professor John S. Mbiti, at the 1976 Pan African Christian Leadership Conference Assembly in Nairobi, gave a definition of culture as

the human pattern of life in response to man's environment, ... expressed in physical forms such as agriculture, arts, technology, in inter-human relations such as institutions, laws, customs and in forms of reflection on the total reality of life such as language, philosophy, religion, spiritual values and world view. (Nicholls 1979, 11)

14

According to Luzbetak, "culture as a design for living is a plan for coping with a particular society's physical, social and ideational environment. It is a complete and more or less successful adaptive system, which includes the total content as well as the organization of the content" (1970, 64).

E. B. Taylor describes culture as "that complex whole which includes knowledge, belief, art, morals, law, customs and any other capabilities and habits acquired by man as a member of society" (Luzbetak 1970, 59). While Lowie defines culture as "the sum total of what an individual acquires from his society, those beliefs, customs, artistic norms, food-habits and crafts which come to him not by his own creative activity but as a legacy from the past conveyed by formal and informal education" (60). Others have tried to define culture in simple terms as "tradition," "total social heredity," and "way of life."

Hiebert defines "culture as the integrated system of learned patterns of behavior, ideas and products characteristic of a society" (1985 25). And Nida explains it as "learned behavior which is socially acquired, that is, the material and nonmaterial traits which are passed on from one generation to another. They are both transmittable and accumulative" (1954, 28). For his part, David J. Hesselgrave defines culture as "the more or less integrated systems of ideas, feelings and values and their associated patterns of behavior and products shared by a group of people who organize and regulate what they think, feel and do" (1991 30).

From the few quotations above, we can see that culture is a very complex and all-inclusive word. It covers social, linguistic, psychological, economic, geographical, and other areas of human life and activity. For the purpose of this book I would like to define it simply as the sum total of learned behavior patterns of individuals that enable them to live and identify themselves as a community. I agree with Luzbetak that,

"culture is a design for living. It is a plan according to which society adapts itself to its physical, social, and ideational environment.

A plan for coping with the physical environment would include such matters as food production and all technological knowledge and skill. Political systems, kinship, family organization and law are examples of social adaptation, a plan according to which one is to interact with his fellows. Man copes with his ideational environment through knowledge, art, science, philosophy, and religion. Cultures are but different answers to essentially the same human problems." (1970, 60)

By careful observation, we will come to realize that the behavior patterns and structures of a community include how they see or perceive the world through their religion, values, government, language, feelings, morals, and law.

G. Linwood Barney defines culture as a series of layers (Nicholls 1979, 11), as you can see in the figure below. The deepest of these layers consists of ideology and worldview. From this first layer comes the formulation of values in the second layer, which influences the institutions such as marriage, law, and education in the third layer. The fourth and outermost layer includes the material artifacts and observable behavior and customs. Although the Barney model has its limitations, it gives us an idea of the base and factors that eventually influence human behavior.

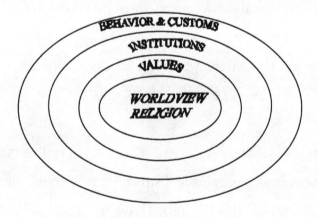

It is true that at the center of every culture is the community's worldview, or the way the people see, understand, and perceive the world around them. In the typical African culture, I put religion and world-view together as they seem inseparable and are the foundation upon which other institutions, values, and customs are built. In the Brong Ahafo Region of Ghana, for instance, one tribe believes that their ancestors came from the ground through a big hole located in the center of the town (a small hut has been built on top of it to protect it). They also believe that their ancestors came on a Tuesday, and because of that, no citizen is expected to work on that day. Tuesday is therefore observed as a market day for the area and is well patronized by people from far and near.

Upon careful observation, it should be noted that not only the above-mentioned group but in most African cultures religious factors dominate almost the entire range of social activities. You can hardly touch any area of life without coming into contact with their religious beliefs and practices.

Another area closely related to worldview and typical of my own culture is our value system. What matters most? The average African culture is people centered; therefore, relationships are more important than anything else. There is a common saying in my language, *"din pa ye sen ahonya,"* which literally means "A good name is better than riches." In other words, it is a warning that we must be careful in acquiring wealth because being wealthy through unacceptable means could have a negative effect on our integrity. Much importance is attached to the name of an individual and even his family unit. While the typical Westerner is more concerned about physical wealth and comfort, we are more concerned about our integrity, name, and what others think. In the West, wealth is determined by business investments, cars, and buildings. In African culture, wealth is measured by *people*, hence the problem of high birth rates. The more wives and children you have, the more respected you are. In fact, barrenness is regarded as a curse in some cultures.

For any society to preserve its identity and continuity, it needs some sort of organization to be able to function and move in unison as a group. Societies are made up of individuals who share the same beliefs and characteristics. They are dependent on one another for growth and survival. They must understand and be able to relate to each other in an orderly way, and so they have a need for language and social structures.

Careful observation will reveal that most African societies, although seen by Westerners as primitive and uncivilized, are well organized and more structured than what an outsider might think. The leadership structure starts with the small family unit and extended family and continues through the local to the paramount chief. Apart from the chiefs and queen mothers (the leaders of the women), there are other offices attached to those of the chiefs and leaders with specific roles. In fact, some families and personalities are assigned specific and permanent roles within the society. For example, with the Akans in Ghana, the "Okyeame" (linguist) is the spokesperson of the chief or king. The "Sanaahene" is the treasurer of the kingdom. The "Queenmother" represents the women in the community, and nominates someone to become the chief when the position becomes vacant. All these are aimed at stability, continuity, security, and the welfare of the community and the individual.

This leads us into the area of behavior and customs. As already mentioned, the average African culture is people centered. The behavior of individuals within the society is therefore carefully considered before assigning any role. A key role within the culture or society would never be assigned to anyone who is likely to behave like a foreigner in their midst. Therefore, everyone must learn to live within the cultural norms of the people.

People are taught how to behave by the culture or family, either formally or informally. Each society has its own way of teaching its young. Parents can discipline their children for behaving contrary to cultural norms, and the community can also punish adults for violating cultural norms. It must be noted, however, that although many of our behavior patterns are learned formally and informally, others are natural and can be observed by people from different cultural backgrounds. These include facial expressions of anger, fear, joy, and sorrow.

Because culture is shared by a number of people,

there is the need for all involved to behave in such a way as to contribute to the welfare of everyone. Each person expects the other member to behave according to their cultural norms to ensure peace, good relationships, and strong community ties.

In their book *Cultural Anthropology: A Christian Perspective*, Stephen A. Grunlan and Marvin K. Mayers (1979, 216–217) mention four factors that produce normative behavior, or reasons for behavior norms. According to them, normative behavior produces maximum satisfaction, the value of predictability, restraint of power, and secondary gains. Although these behavior norms are known to be in the best interest of the individual and community as a whole, they are not always followed by everyone within the community, hence the need for social control mechanisms that include laws.

Although the so-called social and moral laws are not written in most cases, they are passed on from generation to generation verbally and through behavior patterns. They include such areas as proper

23

dress, greetings, marriage, agriculture, trade, and even eating habits, and some are more strictly observed than others. However small the society or group might be, it would also definitely have its own system of government, regulations, and ways of enforcing its legal systems, although they may not have a Western type of police, courts, or other law enforcement agencies.

Culture, therefore, can be described as the sum total of certain beliefs, practices, and institutions to help the people to live. The next chapter will focus on the individual within the culture.

Chapter Two

CULTURE AND THE INDIVIDUAL

The maintenance and self-expression of every culture, including language, is done through its individual members. The individual member of the society is therefore very important in many aspects. He can be said to be the representative or ambassador of the group wherever he goes, and the culture of his people is portrayed through him.

It is interesting to note that as much as the culture of a society is expressed and portrayed to the outside world by the individual, the individual can at times act as a change agent within the community, depending on his role. This does not however belittle the role of group decisions. In other words, while portraying his own culture, either consciously or unconsciously, to the outside world, the individual can be exposed to other cultures, which may influence him. This influence may then lead to a change in his culture, depending on the extent of the influence of the foreign culture and the damage done to his own culture or the percentage of individuals acculturated.

Although the expression and maintenance of the cultural heritage of the people depends on the individual to some extent, that doesn't necessarily make it an individualistic society. Most African societies are structured in such a way as to first protect and serve the community as a whole, but with the individual's welfare at the center. This can be seen in the extended family system, kinship, and strong community ties. The individual is not highly regarded above the society, as in the Western world, but gets his identity from his group and particularly from the role he plays within the group. The most honored and cherished are those who contribute to the well-being of the community, and those individuals are blessed by the community. The idea or belief is to put the interest of the community first, and when the community is well built, strong, and effective, it will in turn be able to protect the individuals and save their interests.

For example, when a chief is installed in my culture, as in most Ghanaian and African cultures, he is made to swear an oath of allegiance expressing his willingness to put the interest of the society above all others, to protect it, and to be obedient to all calls to duty at any time, whether day or night. The people, led by their elders, mainly divisional chiefs and family heads, in turn express their loyalty to the chief and the state. The chief therefore expects the cooperation and loyalty of his people at all times, and the people expect the chief and his elders to protect and serve their interests as a society and individuals. When one member of the society is attacked by someone from another group, it is seen and regarded as an attack on the whole and can lead to a civil war between the two groups.

The idea, therefore, is to pull resources together and build a strong society to enable the society to take proper care of the individual's needs. In other words, the individuals put the society first but expect the leadership and the society to put the individual first in all decision making. The ideology is "Divided we fall; united we stand."

Chapter Three

THE GOSPEL AND CULTURE

Many of our theological differences arise from our cultural backgrounds, for we at times unconsciously confuse our culture with the Word of God and our theology.

Culture, as the lifestyle of a people and how they perceive the world, both physically and spiritually, is aimed at helping the people to live within their community. The Word of God, or the purpose of the Gospel, is to reveal God's plan for human behavior wherever they may find themselves. It is therefore of utmost importance for Christians to recognize that God's purposes can be fulfilled in diverse forms in different cultures, which makes it necessary for us (Christians) to become very familiar with both the Gospel and culture. Our understanding of culture will enable us to apply and relate biblical teachings in a manner consistent to God's purposes, which are universal.

Studying human behavior will help us to know and understand the differences between human beings, especially as social groups. Social groups differ in their structures, value systems, linguistics, dress, behavior norms, worldviews, and in other areas. The differences in our cultures, the cultures we seek to reach or communicate the Gospel to, and the cultural influences of the people through whom the Gospel was communicated to us can at times raise some theological problems. Our "structures," in this context, implies the way we organize and arrange things for the common good of the people.

For example, how marriage is arranged in Ghana (the Akan perspective) differs from what prevails in America. In Ghana, marriage ultimately unites the four families of the couple—the bride's father's and mother's families and the bridegroom's father's and mother's families. One can easily reach Ghanaians, especially those in the rural areas, through their chiefs and those in the religious bodies through their leaders. This is so because the Ghanaian structure demands the people respect and follow their leaders.

Values are collective conceptions of what is considered good, desirable, and proper as well as bad, undesirable, and improper in a culture. Many things considered desirable in Ghana may undoubtedly be undesirable elsewhere. For example, childbearing is of prime importance in the Ghanaian society. And in Ghana, an adult would prefer death to life to avoid stigmatization from his or her people. To work effectively in a Ghanaian community, for that matter in any community, one needs to be conversant with the value system of that group of people.

According to Richard T. Schaefer and Robert P. Lamm, language is an abstract system of word meanings and symbols for all aspects of culture. They describe language as the foundation of every culture, and it includes speech, written characters, numerals, symbols, and the gestures of nonverbal communication (1995, 68). Now, as a result of globalization, people have access to all countries under the sun, and the only serious barrier is language. The language barrier has hampered much progress. If linguistic differences are not understood, the study of human behavior will not be complete.

All societies have ways of encouraging and enforcing what they view as appropriate behavior and discouraging and punishing what they consider to be improper conduct. Norms are established standards of behavior maintained by the society. For example, what someone wears, in the Ghanaian perspective, reflects a person's true motive. Dress should not be taken for granted because it independently portrays the person's innermost being. These behavior norms differ from society to society.

On the other hand, there are universal norms and needs. These universal norms can be regarded as common and understood by all, wherever one may find himself. Norms such as "do not kill" and "greet your neighbor" are universal, though they may be mores and folkways, respectively. Mores are norms deemed highly necessary to the welfare of the society. The violation of mores can lead to severe penalties, as in the case of killing. Folkways are norms that govern everyday behavior. The violation of folkways raises comparatively little concern; greetings are a typical example.

With regard to the universal need, I will therefore agree with Stephen A. Grunlan and Marvin K. Mayers (1979, 43) that "mankind, wherever found on this planet, is both similar and different." Grunlan and Mayers explain their statement with Malinowski's Permanent Vital Sequence. Malinowski's sum basic needs are metabolism (i.e., the need for food, liquid, and oxygen), reproduction, bodily comforts, safety, movement, growth, and health.

It must however be noted that although all humankind have these basic needs, attempts to meet these needs are pursued in different ways by different people. To sustain human life, we eat different things in different ways and even at different times. For the purpose of reproduction, control of sex drive, and survival of a society, each community has its own marriage systems, regulations, and norms. The same goes for the needs for bodily comfort, safety, movement, and health. The end result, or product, of trying to meet these needs is "the agreed and learned community behavior patterns" that ensure peace and harmony.

However, as a result of the fall of man, man's attempt to make life meaningful and worth living has always fallen below God's standards and is at times in direct conflict, at least certain aspects, with God's design and purposes for humankind. In fact, the fall has created a vacuum, which brings dissatisfaction in man that can only be filled by God through the work of Christ Jesus on the cross.

The subject of culture becomes more complex and very complicated at times as there could be subcultural groups within a society that might initially be seen by an outsider as one cultural or homogenous unit. This subculture, according to Schaefer and Lamm (1995) is "a segment of society which shares a distinctive pattern of mores, folkways, and values which differs from the pattern of the larger society."

The universal church, as the Body of Christ, which is and must be one in spirit, transcends these cultural and subcultural groupings. There is only one God and one Gospel, but there are many cultures, languages, behavior patterns, values, beliefs, and structures. In this book I will limit myself to the relationship between the Gospel and culture, church and culture, and generally how Christianity relates to culture.

The purpose of the Gospel is to reveal the love and the nature of God to humankind wherever he might be found, in his own cultural setting. This self-revelation of God may result in the change of behavior patterns of individuals and communities. It has however never been easy for those who are involved in communicating the Gospel, even in one's own cultural setting, because of the complexity of human and individual behavior. The early church, despite the mighty working and presence of the Holy Spirit, was not an exception. If one carefully reads chapter 15 of the Acts of the Apostles, you will begin to see and understand the relationship between culture and the Gospel.

It has been over one hundred and sixty years since the first missionaries set foot in Ghana, yet there are some unanswered questions still facing the Ghanaian church in relation to some cultural practices of the people. Questions such as whether a polygamist or a traditional chief can become a full member of a church and whether traditional drums can be used during worship services are still pending in some denominations.

Some church leaders, in an attempt to indigenize certain aspects of their worship, have been debating the possibility of accepting the pouring of libation as an indigenous form of prayer. They argue that pouring of libation is another form of worship and can be adopted by the Christian community. And some of our African Independent Churches (AIC) in Ghana officially accept polygamy as normal and culturally related under the pretext that some Old Testament (and New Testament 1 Tim. 3:2) God-fearing people were married to more than one wife and were accepted by God. To them, there is no logic or reason why the Western missionary should try to impose his cultural norms on them.

It can be seen that the problem has been and still arises from our misunderstanding of the relationship between the Gospel, our theology, and cultures. God, in his sovereignty, has chosen to use human beings and their cultures as a channel of communicating the Gospel message to humankind, and because of that we shall continue to struggle over these issues from one group of people to another.

As already indicated, culture is the total sum of acquired and shared behavior patterns of a community. These include the ways the people think, feel, do things, and express themselves. What may be regarded as normal in culture A may be quite abnormal in the eyes of culture B, and what may be regarded in culture B as something very important might not be taken note of in culture A simply because they think, see, and value things and people differently. These cultural behavior patterns influence us more than we realize and may at times influence our own understanding and communication with others.

Every culture has its own way of seeing the world around it and determining what to do and not to do. In short, in dealing with culture, one must always bear in mind that it has to do with the ideas, feelings, and values of the community concerned. The Gospel also has to do with ideas, feelings, and values and is effective only as it affects, in one way or the other, these areas of human life and activity.

Before someone is understood to be converted or committed to Christ, he should have heard, understood, and agreed with what the Word of God says about the world, man, and God. Thus, a change of ideas and an understanding about the world and creation is of prime importance and in fact a prerequisite to becoming a Christian. The convert's feelings are touched because of his guilt as a sinner, and when salvation is understood, feelings of joy and peace follow upon the realization of God's grace and love.

God's grace and love can't be properly understood without affecting our lifestyles. They affect our interests, values, priorities—everything. We begin to see the life hereafter in a different way. We are no longer interested in seeking spiritual assistance through our ancestors; we begin to communicate directly with prayers to God through his Son, Jesus Christ. When such a change takes place in the lives of many people within a cultural group at the same time, you can foresee the interactions within the society. It is in this area of changing loyalties between one's culture and what has been called the *supraculture* that the conflict between the Gospel and culture begins to surface.

The Gospel and Christianity demand obedience and loyalty, but our culture also expects our continued loyalty to maintain our membership in the community. To be a beneficiary, one has to also be a contributor. How then can we be loyal and committed to both our communities and our newfound faith?

Sometime ago, I was leading a seminar for pastors in a town a few kilometers from my hometown, and my uncle sent someone to inform me that my senior brother was sick, although my uncle knew that I was neither a medical doctor nor a herbalist. I informed him through the messenger that I was leading a pastors' seminar and that I would come the following day. When I arrived the next day, the first thing he did was to summon a meeting of our extended family. He wanted to know whether I wanted to continue with my membership in the family because of my failure to respond to his immediate call the previous day. In effect, he wanted to make it clear that they wouldn't accept my halfhearted loyalty. He also wanted to know whether I was going to live according to the norms of my newfound faith or our cultural norms.

It can be seen from the incident with my uncle that as much as the Gospel demands a commitment, the community or culture into which someone was born also expects some sort of contribution to keep it going. Anything that seems to threaten their oneness

40

and cooperative efforts may be regarded as a threat to the stability of the whole community and resisted with all available means, which normally begins with the rejection and expulsion of the person or people involved.

The purpose of the Gospel is to reveal the love of God to man. It has a holistic ministry to reach and enable one to know and worship God in his own environment without necessarily crossing cultural barriers. The Gospel by nature is revolutionary, and because of that it can easily be misunderstood. At times, unnecessary barriers may be created if culturally appropriate methods are not used. We need the trust of the community to get their listening ear.

We can't run away from the fact that the Gospel was communicated through the Jewish culture, and there cannot be effective communication without the medium of human culture, as the message is directed to human beings who can only hear it through their cultural language. The message needs to be incarnated to them. Care however must always be taken to give the right distinction between the pure Gospel and cultural elements. The failure of this differentiation by some missionaries has led to people being skeptical about the Gospel and its message, thus creating problems in some areas as mentioned.

One unfortunate area of concern, which will take some time to be redressed, has been the attitude of some Western missionaries who either consciously or unconsciously tried to equate their culture with the Gospel in their cross-cultural communication efforts. Cultural means must be and have been used whenever there is communication of the Gospel, but deliberate attempts should be made to avoid cultural imperialism by bearing in mind that the Gospel is distinct from all cultures. Cultural bridges must be looked for, located, and used.

We must always see the positive relationship between the Gospel and culture. Apart from effective communication, the different cultures could help us in our understanding of God and his relationship with man.

Chapter Four

CHRIST AND CULTURE

Whens it comes to the question of the relationship between Christ and culture, there are different views as to whether to put Christ above culture or put culture at par with him. There are at least five different views generally accepted that are under discussion (Hesselgrave 1991, 116). There are those who see culture as demonic, and because of our commitment to Christ, we should have nothing to do with, or even go near, cultural places. Others believe that Christianity is at par with culture, except that Christianity is better. Some put Christ above culture and regard him as the one who makes it complete.

Others put both on the same level. And finally, there are those who believe that culture is what it is today because of fallen man and in Christ it can be renewed for the better and to God's glory.

But the basic question still remains, which comes first, Christ or Culture? In other words, should Christ or the scriptures be given a higher view over cultural norms? In trying to answer that question, I would like to draw attention to the fact that, despite the fall of man, God has never ceased revealing himself to humankind. You can hardly find a single cultural group without the name of God in their vocabulary. This clearly confirms the fact that God is not only the creator of man but the source of his culture.

God can be seen at work in almost every culture, even before the arrival of the modern missionary in the so-called most primitive areas. I therefore agree with Bruce J. Nicholls that

the assumption of Christianity is that God is the sovereign creator and lord who controls the

44

created world and acts within it according to his own purpose. The culture of the Hebrews was not just the product of their environment but was the interaction of the supra cultural and Hebrews in their environment and history. (1979, 13)

It seems as if we are tempted at times out of holy zeal to unconsciously try to create the impression that we don't have to touch the unholy cultural items and places. Christ himself tried to communicate to the people of his day through culturally appropriate and relevant language and expressions. He never condemned culture; he only condemned certain aspects and practices that were contrary to God's Word and purposes. God took the form of man to be able to speak to us in an appropriate form.

Man cannot be separated from his culture. It is his way of life, identity, and survival. The Lausanne Covenant rightly says,

Because man is God's creature, some of his culture is rich in beauty and goodness. Because he has fallen, all of it is tainted with sin and some of it is demonic. The Gospel does not presuppose the superiority of any culture to another, but evaluates all cultures according to its own criteria of truth and righteousness, and insists on moral absolutes in every culture. The Lausanne Movement: Lausanne Covenant (1974, 10).

Man needs culture to exist. The problem has been the effect of sin on culture.

Chapter Five

THEOLOGY AND CULTURE

Our common calling in our varied cultural situations, as was the calling of earlier generations, is to remain faithful in our commitment to Christ. This is because the content of Christian communication is Christ himself.

Theology deals with this concept and is an attempt to express our experience with God; it is human thinking about God, rather than purely and simply the words and thoughts of God. In other words, theology deals with the study of the relationship between God and his creation, and man is the center of creation. According to Charles R. Taber,

> Confusing theology with God is one form of
> idolatry. Failure to recognize the cultural rela-
> tivity of theology also leads to many problems
> when the effort is made to transpose bodily a
> theology from one cultural setting to another.
> The fact that the subject of theology is super-
> natural-absolute-ultimate does not give these
> properties either to the process or to the find-
> ings of theology, any more than mere talk
> about jokes is itself humorous. (1978)

Theology would be incomplete without relating it to
the total human behavior.

Theology is essentially an attempt to give expression to the experience of an encounter of God in a way
that can explain and justify the experience and make it
accessible to other people. Theology, especially when
it is truly dynamic and valid, is bound to be culturally conditioned in the questions it raises and answers

and in the methodology and terminology it uses. On the one hand, there is the prior enculturation of the people doing theology, and on the other hand, there is a need to communicate the message to people who are themselves enculturated. It is interesting to note that in some circles there is a considerable reluctance to accept the implications of the cultural conditioning of theology. But can we really separate one from the other and be effective in our studies?

The more we study man as a social and spiritual being, the more we should be able to learn about God. The Word of God helps us to understand human origin, and God also uses our social relationships and cultural setting to relate, reveal, and communicate his purposes to us. There is therefore no wonder that God's desire to speak to us came in human form— with a culture—to effectively communicate to us. Theology can therefore not be separated from culture.

Any theology and hermeneutic is and must be profoundly conditioned by the culture in which it arises because those who develop their diverse expressions of faith are themselves conditioned by their own enculturation. It must be this way because they must speak to other persons also profoundly enculturated so as to motivate and transform them.

It has been said that the act of communication, in its essence, automatically and necessarily belongs to a culture, that there are no noncultural media. To be effective, communication must be expressed in verbal and nonverbal cultural language. I am not in any way saying that theology should be formulated around culture. That would definitely bring in syncretism. Instead, all theologies must constantly be brought into subjection or scrutiny of the Word of God.

Chapter Six

THE CHURCH AND CULTURE

In many denominations, you will find three theologies in practice: the official one promulgated
in the constitution, the one being taught in the Bible
school, and the informal one that tacitly informs and
influences the lives of lay people. It becomes more
complex when an attempt is made to reach others
cross-culturally. It is therefore no wonder that another
conflict area, which will continue to face the Christian
worker and the missionary in particular, is the relationship between the church and the host culture and
how to theologically accommodate it.

The church and the Gospel it presents are geared

toward a change. And the question we will always have to answer is, are we to aim at changing the culture of the people as a whole or should we aim at changing certain aspects, and, if so, which particular aspects? I am sure there has not been any simple answer.

Some missionaries, even if not denominations, believe that the church is an agent of culture change as "the light of men" (John 1:4 NKJV). It leads us into "the way, the truth, and the life (John 14:6). We have been called to be agents of change, so no compromise is possible in any way. The whole culture must therefore change for the better.

There is another view that culture is the creation of God, and because of that, it must be respected. Therefore, no attempt should be made toward changing the culture, and the Gospel must then be indigenized to make it acceptable to the people. This attitude I call "extreme accommodation," which will definitely lead to syncretism.

There are those who believe that the Gospel should be put at par with the host culture to make it acceptable to the people. I do not agree with this idea either. I feel that the missionary must be willing to have empathy with the people; understand their culture; act as an insider, although he may not be accepted initially; and be able to identify which areas of the culture are either good or neutral and could possibly be used as bridges.

It has also been argued that "the church cannot change the religion and moral life of a people without changing the particular culture, for if a part is modified, the whole becomes thereby something different, the missionary, therefore is an agent of cultural change" (Luzbetak 1970, 342).

We can't run away from the fact that the church, including the missionary, is an agent of change. But how far and which areas should we aim at? By the way, apart from the church, every culture is undergoing a change in one way or the other, but in different degrees. Some are more rigorous than others. In other words, whether the Gospel is preached or not, changes are taking place and at times for the worse. What then should the church do?

53

I believe that God created man and gave him a cultural mandate, and everything God did was good. There was no problem with man and his culture until the fall. The fall of man affected all areas of life, including his culture. But that doesn't mean that he ceased to have a culture. Again, I will not agree with those who believe that because of the fall of human-kind, all cultures, especially those of the so-called primitive people, are sinful. In every culture, whether African, Asian, American, Indian, black, yellow, or white, there are aspects that are good, neutral, and bad if judged by the Word and nature of God. We have no right to use one culture to judge the other; they all have their own problems. Deliberate attempts must therefore be made constantly to know which aspects of the particular host culture should be accommodated or not. I will like to mention here, however, that, if proper care is not taken, accommodation can bring in its own problems, including syncretism.

One may ask, how far then should we go in accom-modation? I will say that we should go in as far as the

Word and nature of God allow us. Love and justice demand that we respect and accommodate the views and lifestyles of other people. The fact that they are different from us doesn't necessarily mean that they are evil or inferior. A culture can be and is usually more rich and beautiful than could be seen from outside at a glance.

The church and the missionary can only be effective tools in the hand of God by learning to see people as God sees them and by identifying with them. A real bond of trust can only be established through proper accommodation and empathy. I am in no way in favor of compromise, and in fact, if anything I will be against it. All that I want to say is that an Akan, Xhosa, or Zulu should be encouraged to become a Christian in his own cultural context, to be with his own people without unnecessarily trying to cross cultural barriers.

To me, accommodation is simply trying to meet the other halfway to be able to communicate effectively with the other person. He may not understand, accept, or even hear you if you do not. I therefore agree with Dr. Louis J. Luzbetak that "accommodation calls for an adjustment in altitude, outward behavior and approach also in regard to the peculiar structuring of the local life-way" (1970, 846).

Again, I want to reiterate that accommodation doesn't mean that the church should accept everything in the native or local culture. It must not compromise the pure seed of the Gospel. The Gospel message is universal, but the channels of communication and the recipients are not, hence the need for accommodation of each other. Accommodation is trying to identify and have empathy, as much as possible, to be able to communicate effectively for the required results without humiliating the other person or group. It is accepting them as they are to be able to get their acceptance and cooperation in return.

Experience has shown that as the pure word is sown in the hearts and lives of people, they begin to ask or desire that certain practices within their culture that are contrary to the Word of God be changed. The target of the Gospel must be seen as the inward, not the outward. The outward must only be seen as the evidence of what has taken place inwardly.

In talking about accommodation, we should not forget that the church has human elements incorporated in institutions or the constitution. These include the order of service, music, buildings, dress, and celebrations. These external appearances and expressions should not be superimposed on the people, thus denying them the opportunity to take part in the establishment of a church they can later identify as their own.

Apart from ethnocentrism—the tendency to assume that one's culture and way of life are superior to all others—and the influence of the sending church, one major hindrance to accommodation is the feeling of superiority and know-it-all attitude of the missionary. As Luzbetak said,

A missionary whose mind is completely occupied with the "pagan" culture's "falsehood," "immorality," "darkness," "depravation," and "blindness" who sees among his adopted people nothing but "spiritual misery," sin, and "the night of heathenism"—such a missionary ought to have his spiritual eyes examined. (1970, 352)

Eugene A. Nida has also commented on this:

Perhaps in the matter of esthetic culture more than in any other area of life, Christian missions have usually unintentionally, stifled indigenous practices. For the most part missionaries have assumed that those habits of worship, which are approved in their own home churches, have universal validity. Even the order of service becomes for many a matter of doctrine. All this is quite unfortunate, for too often the indigenous esthetic resources have been denounced. The ethnocentric principle of transplanting churches has overruled the Biblical principal of sowing the seed. (1954, 195)

Christian workers are change agents, who should not allow their ethnocentrism to hinder the effective communication of the Gospel. We have to look for the good and neutral aspects of the culture in which ourselves and make good use of them.

Chapter Seven

THE CHALLENGE OF COMMUNICATION

O f Ghana's population of over 24 million, 69 percent claim to be members of a Christian church. However, a national church survey compiled in 1989 revealed that only 11percent of the national population attends a church on regular basis on an average Sunday. The average church attendance differs in most cases from one region to the other. Ghana has been divided into ten regions in the chart below. The attendance ranges between 15 percent in the southern part of the country to 3 percent in the less-developed and poorer north. Below is the summary of religious affiliation and practice by regions in 1989(National Church Survey).

REGIONS	CHRISTIANS				OTHER RELIGIONS
	Attending Church	Not Attending Church		Total	
Western	14%	67%	898,200	81%	19%
Central	13%	63%	783,700	76%	24%
Greater Accra	15%	63%	1,094,200	78%	22%
Eastern	14%	59%	1,097,400	73%	27%
Volta	10%	52%	693,500	62%	38%
Ashanti	15%	59%	1,406,950	74%	26%
Brong Ahafo	10%	48%	682,200	58%	42%
Northern	3%	7%	99,500	10%	90%
Upper West	6%	13%	62,900	19%	81%
Upper East	3%	5%	46,450	8%	92%
All Regions	11%	49%	6,865,000	60%	40%

Source: Ghana Evangelism Committee (1989), National Church Survey

This survey revealed that four major groups of people were not effectively being reached with the Gospel: seven million nominal Christians (49 percent of the population), fifteen thousand unchurched towns and villages (i.e., villages and towns with no church of any type), almost five million unreached northern and alien people, and the adherents of Islam (15 percent of the population).

Since this church survey, a lot of questions have arisen and several answers have also been given in an attempt to explain the causes of nominalism after over 160 years of the presence of the church in the country. Some of the reasons given include changing social patterns, inadequate churches and church facilities, content and quality of the church's ministry, lack of concern for the lost, inadequate biblically balanced ministry, content not life related, no social concern, lack of vision, and many more.

One very important but neglected area, which needs serious consideration, is in the area of effective cross-cultural communication and contextualization of the Gospel. For effective communication to take place, one needs to consider the context into which he is trying to work. In other words, the way of life of the people, the knowledge of the people about the world around them, the way they think, and their language, value system, general beliefs, and lifestyles must be taken into consideration.

Chapter Eight

UNDERSTANDING THE PEOPLE'S WORLDVIEW

I t is a fact that most Africans, if not all, believe in the existence of a Supreme God. Their knowledge and worship of this Supreme Being, however, may vary from tribe to tribe and from country to country.

The Mende people of Sierra Leone are said to believe in a Creator God called "Ngewo." He is believed to have existed from the beginning and is author of all life of visible and invisible spirits. In Nigeria, the Yoruba people call God "Olurun," which means "owner of all of the sky." He is believed by all as the Creator of all things, the "All Mighty" and "All

Knowing," the giver of life and breath, and the final judge of all men.

The Ashanti (Akan) in Ghana, if not all Ghanaians, believe that the universe is full of spirits. They also believe that there is a Supreme Being who created all things and manifests his power in diverse ways. Some, however, hold the belief that God, being supreme, or a king, can be better approached through other lesser spirits, which animate trees, animals, rivers, stones, and other objects. There are also the ever-present spirits of the ancestors (*Nsamanfo*) who can help through their contacts with the world of the spirits. The Ashanti conception of the Supreme Being may be gathered from the titles ascribed to him. For example, he is known as the "Dependable One" (*Twereduampon*), the "Powerful One" (*Otumfour*), and the "One who Satisfies" (*Onyame*).

According to a well-known myth in Ghana, long ago, God lived very near to men, in the sky. There was also a certain old woman who used to pound her fufu (a meal) made of mashed yam, plantain, or cocoyam, and whenever she did so, the long pestle she used knocked against God (Onyame), who lived in the sky, very close to man. So one day God said, "Because of what you have been doing to me, I am moving away, far up into the sky, where men cannot reach me." So he went up into the sky, and men could no longer approach him. Apart from the titles and myths, references in almost every Ghanaian culture attest to their beliefs and how they perceive the world around them and the one who created it in songs, proverbs, and riddles in archaic grammatical forms.

The Ashanti and other tribes in Ghana, like most African tribal communities, believe not only in the existence of a Supreme Being but also in the existence of a world of spirits where their ancestors live a life similar to the life on earth. This concept comes clear during funeral rites. The dead are given food, drink, bedding, clothing, ornaments, cash, and other items to help them on their journey to the world of spirits. It is believed that they will need the items, so they are buried with them.

An Ashanti, or average Ghanaian unbeliever, has his ancestors in mind constantly. They are believed to be always watching over their living relatives. They punish those who break the customs or fail to fulfill their obligations to their kinfolk. To such people, they send misfortune and illness or even death. There has been constant circulation of stories in villages and towns of deaths believed to have been caused by the intervention of ancestors, and priests of the gods (witch doctors) also often declare that an ancestor, because of some guilt or misconduct on the part of the sufferer, has caused sickness or even barrenness. On the other hand, those who obey the laws, customs, worship, and who fulfill their obligations receive the help and blessing of the ancestors. They see to it that the crops of such people are plentiful, that children are born to them, and that their undertakings prosper.

In some areas, each lineage or extended family has its own family stool, which is the shrine of its ancestors. Sometimes it is apart from the community's shrine. On this family shrine, the head of the family or clan, at the appropriate season, offers food and drinks to the ancestors, praying that they may protect members of that family and bless them with health, long life, children, and good yield of food and crops.

To the average Ghanaian unbeliever or African in general, disease and death are untimely caused by spirit powers. As stated earlier, they believe the universe is full of spirits, which for one reason or the other may act for or against man. There is no doubt that God is held very high in the thinking of Africans. However, problems arise whenever there is an attempt to compare nonexistent gods to God the creator of the Bible.

Chapter Nine

GOD AND THE GODS

The tension between God and the other gods is reflected in all cultures with an animistic heritage. The issue however is the nature of the Creator God and his demand for our wholehearted allegiance and worship. The people of Israel, who were polytheistic in Egypt, had to learn the hard way that Yahweh was the Incomparable One because of his deliverance and miracles they had seen. They were able to say later "Who is like unto thee …?" (Exod. 15:11 KJV).

I agree with Gailyn Van Rheenen that "gods have become the fronts for demons. In a sense idols are no gods because human hands carved them. These gods have power only because they are used by demons" (1 Cor. 10:20; 1 Cor. 7:4; 1 Thess. 1:9; Gal.4:8) (1991, 112). In our attempt to communicate the gospel cross-culturally, efforts must be made through the study and understanding of how far these animistic beliefs are entrenched, either consciously or unconsciously, in the lives and hearts of individuals and communities to be able to relate the Gospel effectively to them.

From the beginning, the Gospel and its demands of total commitment and single-mindedness must be made clear using the appropriate cultural language, which will make it understandable. We must admit, however, that when we examine animistic societies and their beliefs, we see that they are more responsive to the Gospel than people in the so-called Western civilized world. This confirms that God was at work within the cultures even before the arrival of the missionary, and that it is the missionary's task to build upon or continue from where the people in the society are. It must be made clear who the true God is, how incomparable and jealous he is, his distinctiveness, and his other attributes. As Van Rheenen explains, "God is unique among the spiritual beings of the world and therefore, must be given undivided loyalty. His holiness and greatness are a contrast to the moral ambivalence of lower gods" (1991, 270).

God must be presented in a clear and culturally meaningful way as the one who is living not distant from us and as one who desires an intimate and personal fellowship with his followers. God is concerned with our everyday lives.

Chapter Ten

WORSHIP

As already indicated, God is held very high in the thinking of the African, and this can be seen in the study of the various names, praises, and attributes ascribed to God. He is known as the one on whom "you lean and do not fall," "one who responds when called," the one "who has always been there," and the one who "hidden but sees everything," and many more.

In the Akan tradition, God is seen as the ultimate and that nothing is done or happens unless he has allowed it. This is a deterministic belief that is also found among several African peoples. It is also believed that at the creation of man God gives him his destiny (*nkrabea*), which will dictate his mode of life. This of course is an expression of God's overriding sovereignty; he creates and governs life. However, some of these same people hold the belief that there are in fact two destinies, the one given by God and another chosen by the individual himself. The placing side by side of these two destinies is evidently a way of saying that man is, despite God's sovereignty, accountable for his actions.

The average African is very much aware of the existence of a Supreme Being and the invisible or spiritual world, and he sees them as part of the universe. He also believes that the physical world is controlled by the spiritual world; therefore, acts of worship are performed to keep alive the contact between the visible and invisible worlds, between men and God. However, he also feels inadequate, very small, powerless, and insignificant in the sight of God. So in approaching God, he sometimes needs the help of someone else, just as it is often the custom to approach someone of a high status through someone else. Some Africans, therefore, deem it fit to approach God through intermediates, which may be human beings, fetish priests or mediums.

The use of intermediates as a means of reaching God is found in most African societies. They feel that they cannot or should not approach God alone or directly and must do so through the mediation of special persons, other beings, or mediums. The reason for this feeling and practice derives mainly from the social life of different African communities. For example, it is the custom of the Ashanti in Ghana to approach their king or chief indirectly through the intermediary of a linguist (known as *okyeame*), the official spokesman of the chief, through whom the chief also communicates to his subjects. The linguist is very close to the chief and sometimes acts for him during the chief's absence. There are, however, occasions when people could approach the chief directly, such as in the case of an emergency.

In some tribes, there are full-time fetish priests

and priestesses in charge of their smaller gods. Before someone becomes a priest or priestess, he or she is trained and then initiated and consecrated. In Ghana, this may take between one and five years. Priestly duties include performing the daily or weekly rites, the offering of prayers for blessings for the barren and other needy persons, and the pouring of libation to the ancestors. Duties also include offering of sacrifices, conducting both private and public ceremonies, and caring for the shrines or temples, thus fulfilling the office as a religious intermediary between men and God. In some societies, the priests have also political duties, which vary from tribe to tribe.

Prayer is the most common way of approaching God, and this is done in most, if not all, the African societies. People may pray as individuals or as family heads. Prayers are also made communally at public meetings and for public purposes. Despite the belief that anyone can pray to God directly, at any time and any place, some of the prayers and rites are done through the priests, chiefs, and heads of families.

Worship, which includes prayer, sacrifices, and offerings, takes place at appointed seasons and places. The religious calendar is thus of great importance for the worshipping community because communities associate worship with critical times in the life of the society. The hunting, fishing, planting, harvesting, and putting up of new buildings are of special importance. The beginning of the year, week, and day and at the new moon are viewed as auspicious times for acts of worship.

In most societies, the worship of spirits and gods is neither formal nor regular. Acts of worship include sacrifices and offerings of gifts to the gods in exchange for gifts received or anticipated. They include offerings devoted to the gods, which are sacrifices intended to avert the wrath of the gods or to express the worshippers complete dependence upon them in the ensuing years. In some cases, the sacrifices or offerings are supposed to be made to God through the gods or spirits.

Chapter Eleven

SACRIFICES AND OFFERINGS

In African societies, life is closely associated with blood, as in the scriptures. Life is regarded to be in the blood. When blood is being shed, it means life is being poured out. When blood is shed in making a sacrifice, it means that life is being offered to the gods to ask for either forgiveness or protection. Usually such sacrifices are made when the life of a person or a community are in danger. The sacrifice of an animal, such as a fowl, sheep, cow, or goat, is made in the belief that when the sacrifice is accepted or pleasing to the gods, it will help save the life of the person or community, whichever the case may be.

Situations that call for sacrifices may include drought, epidemics, war, and continuous deaths. When they affect the community, it is the community that sacrifices the animal, and every member is expected to contribute to help meet the cost. For personal and family needs, animals are usually used. Such family and personal needs may concern health, marriage, building a new house, business, and remembering (but not worshipping) the ancestors. Again, animals such as sheep, goats, fowls, and even eggs are used.

Chapter Twelve

THE MISSIONARY ROLE: THE WORD OF GOD AND CULTURE

There are quite a number of bridges in the African traditional worldview that could be used in communicating the Gospel effectively and making it more meaningful. The bridges include the belief in the Supreme Being as the Creator, life after death, worship, and sacrifices, to name a few. I believe that the average African communities are more open and responsive to the Gospel than their Western counterparts.

But if someone is to be able to effectively communicate the Gospel cross-culturally, he must begin by getting into the people and their culture as a learner so that he will be able to understand the real and deep meanings of the various beliefs, practices, symbols, and values. To me, the major cause of nominalism and syncretism is the lack of interest and understanding of the people's cultural beliefs and worldview by the missionaries.

The Western missionary comes in and sees the people as without religion, uneducated, or primitive and then tries to present Christianity or religion encapsulated in the missionary's own cultural norms and behavior patterns. The people try to listen to the missionary and accept what he has to offer as a sign of respect and to test it in the light of their worldview, cultural norms, beliefs, and values to see whether it works. If they find it unreliable and not life related, they subtly return to their traditional ways of finding solutions to their problems. Is this because the Gospel lacks the power to meet their spiritual needs or is it due to a lack of interest and understanding on the part of the host culture?

It is a fact that despite the belief of the average African in the existence of a Supreme Being, life after death, and the spiritual world, although not too far away, he has yet to come to the true knowledge and understanding of the Gospel and its implications, like people in other cultures. Their worship, which includes sacrifices and offerings, clearly contradicts the Word of God, although they might be sincere. As Paul rightly said, "I urge you, brothers, in view of God's mercy, to offer your bodies as living sacrifices, holy and pleasing to God – this is your spiritual act of worship." (Romans 12:1 NIV Translation, Zondervan 1985).

Biblical worship must be expressed in our love and gratitude to God in a real act of inward spiritual worship and can be direct to God himself, which is not prevalent in the traditional worship. The Bible clearly states that Christ is the only mediator between God and man and that there is no other way or name through which man can either try to reach God or be saved. To invest any other with this prerogative, therefore, is to assail the unique honor that belongs to Christ. The acceptance of the true believer's worship and service springs from the virtue and efficacy of Christ's mediation, and nothing is a spiritual worship or sacrifice except as rendered through Christ.

In the Bible, Jesus is seen as God's son and man's liberator and Savior in a messianic sense. Because his death is the sacrifice for all sin, raised and seated at the right hand of God, he is the only mediator between God and men. The traditional religions have ideas of mediation, but these in no way approximate the biblical presentation of Christ's priestly ministries and atonement for believers and the world in general.

The African worldview of the Supreme Being, life after death, and worship, including sacrifices and offerings, must only be used and regarded as redemptive analogies or bridges to effectively communicate the Gospel to the practitioner and not to be taken in any way as another way of worshipping the true God.

In Ghana and other African countries, there are inscriptions on cars and lorries such as, "Have faith in God," "Jesus saves," "Everything by God," "God will provide," and "Except God," but acknowledgement of the existence of God and some of his attributes without real commitment or submission to his word, will, and Lordship should not be mistaken as a substitution for the true worshipping of God, which is spiritual.

Although some elements of mysticism are involved and can be seen in the African traditional religion, their main concern is neither to seek to know God nor to become like him. They are more concerned with the immediate or practical benefits than the spiritual. Because of the emphasis on morality, sin is seen only as against the community or an individual, according to their own norms, values, and moral standards, and not against God, as implied in the Bible.

Chapter Thirteen

BRIDGES OF COMMUNICATION

Some of the early missionaries who came to Ghana tried to neglect or explain away the belief and influence of spiritual beings. Others regarded it as something psychological. To them, the main issue is to become a church member and to forget about those things. Many of the missionaries did not see the need to talk about spiritual warfare, as it was nonexistent. Why worry about something not real and only imaginary or psychological? Although a lot could have been learned from the life and ministry of our Lord and Savior Jesus Christ. The early Christians saw

Christian commitment as a life-and-death venture; to them, it was a real warfare, spiritually and, at times, physically.

In fact, Christians and animistic societies relate to personal spiritual beings, but in different ways. While Christians seek to relate to God through Christ as a personal, intimate fellowship and worship, the animists think of a personal relationship between God and man as totally impossible. So they do not try or even think of that possibility. Instead, they try through various means and mediums to manipulate and coerce lower spiritual beings.

The average African does not see the difference between the spiritual and physical or material. To talk about the future, you have to think of the *now* first. To them, if God is close and is concerned about the future, then he should be concerned about our today too. Their attitude is not a rejection of God in their way of thinking, but another means of trying to help themselves. For the missionary to be able to communicate effectively in such a situation, he must try to avail himself with the victory over demonic forces that has been assured in Christ's triumph over death and Satan that is available in his name to those who believe in him.

The love of God, his omnipresence, and his concern should be communicated, incarnated, or lived in their context. The Ghanaian society is more concerned about what we do rather than what we say, hence the need for the missionary to allow himself to be used by the Lord for the Gospel to be lived or incarnated through him. In fact, it would be far better to start living it and building relationships, in other words, bonding or winning the respect and confidence of the people, before verbal communication.

The fatherhood and kingship of God and his desire for undivided loyalty must be stressed. As a father, he has the ability to take proper care of all of his children who sincerely come to him in repentance and genuine faith, relying wholeheartedly on him and forsaking all others. This message must be presented or encoded in a culturally relevant language in such a way that the host culture will be able to understand the difference between God and the gods. It must be presented in such a way that the world sees the supremacy of God as King of Kings, the final judge, the source of life and power, one who knows and understands us, not only as human beings and societies, but as individuals too, and the one who cares.

It is interesting to note that although the belief in life after death is there, what happens after death is unimaginable and simply regarded as joining the living dead or going back to where we came from. The missionary therefore should make good use of the fact that the scriptures are the only reliable source of information on life after death.

The fact and symbol of God's great sacrifice of his only Son to cleanse us of all sin and to deliver us from the powers of Satan must also be communicated. And not only does God love us, he took the initiative in searching for us. He broke into human history in the ministry and death of Christ to break the chains of the wicked one—Satan. Christ has disarmed the powers and authorities. The Gospel message is about liberation—liberation from the demonic forces against which we are fighting. In fact, I think the average African knows more of the reality of spiritual warfare than do most theological students of the West.

One important area that needs the attention of the cross-cultural communicator is social structure and behavior patterns. For example, in Ghana, and in the northern part of the country in particular, most of the people can be effectively reached through the chief or head of the family. In other words, the Western individualistic approach is not as effective in the north and rural communities as in the southern urban areas and cities. The chief has a very important role within the social structure of the rural community. In most of the rural communities, all major decisions are either taken or initiated from chief's palace in cooperation with his elders. It is therefore culturally appropriate to begin from the top—with the leadership.

Because of the importance of culture in communication, I do agree with Gailyn Van Rheenen that,

> The missionary must become a culture learner in order to perceive cultural diversity. He must learn to look beyond superficial similarities to perceive the distinctive ways in which people pattern their cultural reality. These distinctive patterns of reality are worldviews—models of reality that shape cultural allegiances and provide interpretations of the world. Animistic perspectives become comprehensible to the missionary only when he understands the worldviews that validate and integrate cultural values and behavior.
>
> Effective missionaries must accept two presuppositions about worldviews. Worldviews are so natural to insiders that they feel that all others perceive reality their way. Worldviews are like the air we breathe, very important but taken for granted. They are like eyeglasses—not

important until they are lost. Since worldviews are largely implicit, the missionary must search for forums where the implicit is made explicit and develop methodologies for uncovering worldview meanings. (1991, 33)

The missionary, as a learner must look for the bridges of communication in every culture. This will make communication effective and relevant to the targeted group. He should try to take them from the known to the unknown, using culturally relevant illustrations.

CONCLUSION

Culture is a legacy transmitted from generation to generation. It is however not transmitted biologically. It is acquired through learning, either consciously or unconsciously. The term *encultura-tion* is used to describe the learning process, which takes place through various means, including through one's parents, teachers, elders, and friends, and can be formal or informal. Culture can only be said to be biologically acquired in the sense that because we were born into a particular family and community, and as our teaching and learning process has to take place within a community, we easily and naturally accept what comes from our parents, relatives, friends, and eventually our community as the best of everything.

This learning process is believed to begin immediately after birth.

Because everyone is born into a particular culture, there is no person without a culture. As we grow, we become enculturated into the lifestyle and behavior patterns of that particular culture. We act the way we do because we learned and tried to imitate earlier members of our societies. We all like to do things the way we see others act, especially our parents, and that eventually leads us into believing that it is the natural and best way. We even go to the extent of judging the behavior of others through our own community eyes as either right or wrong, which the anthropologists call *ethnocentrism*. In fact, we are all affected by ethnocentrism more than we may realize.

It is very easy to look at how someone behaves, dresses, and thinks and then judge him outright as uncivilized or immature. The main reason can be simply because he is different from us. We should not forget that others may be looking at and judging us too.

It is true that we all naturally like to eat and sleep,

but we have different eating and sleeping habits. While the Westerner may like to have his afternoon siesta and some sort of rest and refreshment, he would be regarded as a lazy person in the African culture. While the Westerner would prefer to use cutlery for meals and regard it as normal, others would regard it as unhygienic but regard using the hand as more hygienic. They would argue that cutlery is washed only once, that is, after use, but they wash their hands before and after meals.

It is very interesting to work with different people groups. One thing I have personally observed in doing is that almost everyone (i.e., cultural group) feels pride about his culture, regards it as the best, and tries to look down on the others. Even what we might be tempted to regard as the most primitive or backward may criticize and abhor certain aspects of the culture we cherish and regard as civilized.

Culture is the self-identity of the people group. It is the verbal and nonverbal ways of self-expression of the people. It is passed on from one generation to another and therefore undergoes changes constantly as a result of internal and external influence. It is no wonder that many African traditional leaders promote the need for cultural revivalism.

To the African traditional leader, a society ceases to exist when it loses its culture. In other words, a society without a culture is no society and is not respected. Because of that belief, many traditional and political leaders have been pursuing different programs aimed at taking the present generation, especially the youth, back to their roots.

I saw an interesting panel discussion on African culture on SABC-TV on June 20, 1993. During this discussion, it was alleged that, although some of the white missionaries came with the best possible intentions, because they didn't understand the people they either completely destroyed or adulterated the people's culture. Thus, the religious beliefs and self-esteem of the people were destroyed. They have been alienated from their culture and self-identification in an attempt to bring them into the world and its culture.

There is therefore a need to revive African conscious-
ness and traditional beliefs.

In Ghana, there have been cultural programs of
late on the national television and radio titled *Sankofa*,
which literally means "go and take it." In other words,
"let's return to our roots to discover our identity as
a society." The symbol of the *Sankofa* programs is a
bird that is looking backward. To the average African
traditional leader, most of our problems have arisen
as a result of the neglect of our traditional beliefs
and practices. In fact, this can be partially true. Yes,
our available resources such as clothes, drums, food,
and many others in our schools, churches, and social
gatherings may not decrease or increase our spiritual
and material development. To the contrary, practicing
what is against the will of God, such as idolatry, will
bring God's curse upon the land.

Finally, in summing up, I would again say that
culture is the sum total of learned behavior patterns
of individuals, which enable them to live and identify
themselves as a community. These learned behavior

patterns include their worldview, religion, values, linguistics, institutions, customs, and laws. Because cultures are learned, they change through internal and external influence. It is therefore to the advantage of the Christian to learn and know how and why these changes take place and how these opportunities could be used as bridges for effective ministry.

At time, we forget that the prime concerns of most cultures are religious and moral issues, and these are the very issues that the Gospel seeks to address. It is therefore in our interest to try to acquaint our-selves with what others think. According to Louis J. Luzbetak, "nothing could be more fundamental than a proper understanding of the term. A failure to grasp the nature of culture would be a failure to grasp much of the nature of missionary work itself" (1970, 59).

God created humankind in his own likeness. He told them to multiply, be fruitful, and to subdue and fill the earth (Gen. 1:26–28). The divine commands are the origins of culture as they include the control of nature, our environment, and the appropriate social organization. The use of our creative powers was to be for the glory of God and to serve others.

However, as a result of the fall, all areas of human behavior became affected and tarnished by sin. Therefore no culture can claim perfection, and the beauty of culture can no longer be seen. Because of the fall of man, evangelists regard everything done outside Christendom as sinful, including culture. Some would therefore have nothing; everything should be completely changed to be Christian.

We should never forget that man has never lived and cannot live without culture. Wherever men have lived, there has been a cultural element of creativity that reflects the Creator. Culture is simply defined as the way of life of a people. Cultural behavior patterns are acquired from childhood, and there is no one without culture.

God's self-disclosure to man was done through people and their culture. He spoke and still speaks through the language, both verbal and nonverbal, so that they can understand. Apart from the fact that

God's self-revelation was done through a culture, we can't communicate outside of culture. No effective communication can be done outside the cultural factor. People at times resist the Gospel, not because they hate it, but because of the improper use of cultural language, either consciously or unconsciously. There is therefore the need for Gospel communicators to appreciate and have empathy with those they seek to reach. Cultural bridges should be looked for and used. Do not forget the need for genuine accommodation.

I wrote this book as an African, because of my interest and concern in cross-cultural communication. Cultural issues, which can hinder the effective communication of the Gospel cut across continents. The following is just an example.

An interview that Ezra Sargunam of the Evangelical Church of India had with the *Global Church Growth* magazine (Oct.–Dec. 1985, 49):

A workable concept of caste is that, it is a necessary evil for function of society in India. Without it, the entire social structure would disintegrate. I agree with the long-term missionary in India who said that caste was misunderstood by westerners. Caste is brotherhood. Caste imposes moral discipline and meets the needs of its members. It offers a sense of belonging. Caste gives Indians a satisfaction that many Americans derive from belonging to fraternal orders or clubs. Exclusion from caste is the worst disaster that can befall an Indian. The Evangelical Church of India would find no purpose served by declaring war on caste. It's just too much for most Hindus to give up caste as a prerequisite to becoming Christian.

A gesture, which is good in one community, may be wrong in another. We must learn to respect other cultures. Our perception might change when we begin to understand them.

It is a fact that most Africans, like Ghanaians, believe in the existence of a Supreme God. They believe that the universe is full of spirits. There is a world of spirits where their ancestors live a life almost similar to life on earth. There is no doubt that God is held very high in their thinking; however, a problem arises whenever there is an attempt to compare other nonexistent or manmade gods to God the Creator of the Bible.

There are bridges in the African traditional world-view, particularly in the Ghanaian society, that could be used to communicate the Gospel effectively. The bridges include the belief in the Supreme Being, life after death, worship, and sacrifice. It is a fact that, despite the belief in the Supreme Being as the Creator, life after death, and the spiritual world, they are yet to come to the true knowledge of the Gospel and its implications. Their worship, which includes sacrifices and offerings, clearly contradicts the Word of God, however sincere they might be.

Biblical worship must be a real act of inward

spiritual worship directed to God. Christ is the only way and mediator between God and man. The traditional religions and worldviews have ideas of mediation, but there is no way that approximates the biblical presentation of Christ's priestly ministries.

The missionary must try to get into the host culture, as much as possible, to be accepted and be able to communicate effectively. He must take the learner-servant role to be able to relate to them. He must look for bridges of communication within the culture and then use them effectively.

BIBLIOGRAPHY

Ghana Evangelism Committee. *National Church Survey.* 1989.

Global Church Growth. October–December, 1985.

Grunlan, Stephen A., and Marvin K. Mayers. *Cultural Anthropology: A Christian Perspective.* Grand Rapids, MI: Zondervan Publishing House, 1979.

Hiebert, Paul G. *Cultural Anthropology.* Baker Book House, 1976.

———. *Anthropological Insights for Missionaries.* Baker Book House, 1985.

Hesselgrave, David J. *Communicating Christ Cross-Culturally.* Zondervan Publishing House, 1991.

Luzbetak, Louis J. *The Church and Cultures.* Techny, Illinois, Divine Word Publications, 1970.

103

Nicholls, Bruce J. *Contextualization: A Theology of Gospel and Culture*. Inter Varsity Press, 1979.

Nida, Eugene A. *Customs and Cultures*. William Carry Library, 1954.

Rheenen, Van Gailyn. *Communicating Christ in Animistic Contexts*. Baker Book House, 1991.

Schaefer Richard T. and Lamm Robert P. *Sociology*, New York, McGraw-Hill, 1995.

Taber, Charles R. *Gospel in Context*. January 1978.

The Lausanne Movement, *Lausanne Covenant* 1974.

CPSIA information can be obtained
at www.ICGtesting.com
Printed in the USA
BVHW091211220523
664632BV00011B/236

9 781625 095466